Introducing Cedrick

The Passionate Poet

Copyright © 2021 Cedrick Lamond Hawkins

Contact: Cedrick Lamond Hawkins
Email: cedrickhawkins@gmail.com
Podcast: CedTalks

RCS Publishing, Leah G. Reynolds
Rcspublishingandmediagrp.com

Pas·sion
intense, driving, or overmastering feeling
or conviction

Table of Contents

Foreword

There comes a time in every young adult's life where he or she must face the terrifying question; *what do you want to do in life?* I asked Cedrick this question one day during his senior year as our AP European History class came to an end.

His response was simple and genuine; *I just want to help and inspire others.* As a high school teacher, I was immediately drawn to his words. It was the first of our many powerful conversations that always seem to converge on the same topics; learning, teaching, and making a positive impact on those around you.

Words can be powerful. When words are written with passion, conviction, and critical thought, they can empower. When words are read with an open mind, they can inspire.
The author has been empowered through his writing. I admire Cedrick's courage to share his most personal thoughts and reflections with the world.

I hope you find inspiration in Cedrick's work. As you emerge yourself into his words, you will grow to know and understand him on a personal level. Through times of triumph, he carries himself with humility and recognizes those who support him. When faced with adversity, he approaches each challenge as an opportunity to grow. During periods of uncertainty, he remains determined. And when he ponders his purpose in life, the answer remains the same; *to help and inspire others.*

-Pete Kerwin

Cedrick's High School Teacher and Mentor

Dedication

I want to dedicate my first novel in loving memory of my father, Lamond Hawkins. I love you Dad.

Introduction

Allow me a moment to introduce myself. I am Cedrick, the Passionate Poet. Through my experiences with life, love, and art I have found a way to express my feelings in the form of words.

Verses that have poured out of my heart like the overflow of emotions spilling from my soul, seeking a place to puddle.

This deep well of emotion and thought have formed into a collection of art that I invite you to experience.

Welcome to my literary home.

Acknowledgments

To my Mom, Leah, Nana (Paulette Creek), Nana (Joyce Hawkins), Dad (Clifton Creek), Pop Pop (Charles Hawkins), and Sean. Thank you for being my biggest supporters, providing for me, and giving me encouragement when I need it the most.

A letter to 16 Year Old Me

Dear Ced,

I know it seems hard right now,
but you have the strength to make it.
You are so smart, and so intelligent,
So please don't let your peers, conform the mind
that you have.

Don't worry about the little things,
for I I struggle with that now.
A smile will come across your perfect face,
When you see what life will bring to your future.

You are creative.
You are a vessel.
You are a teacher.
You are a leader.

You are a black king.
You are a child of the most high God.
Be proud of what you were created to be,
And please stand out among your group.

Never give up and please don't quit,
I promise that your future will be so bright.
You are anointed and you are a blessing,
To the lives that you will touch, as you walk among
your path.

Don't be afraid to fail,

This is something I struggle with now.
For failings are lessons,
That eventually turn to blessings.

Love yourself.
Love your emotions.
Love your body.
Love your complexion.

Love your smile.
Love your nose.
Who cares how you walk?
Your critics could never walk a mile in the shoes
that you fill.

Keep on walking,
And keep on talking.
Keep on knocking,
And keep on rocking.

You heart is filled with gold,
Don't let anyone tell you different.
Continue to walk the path that you're on,
And God will forever bless you with prosperity.

I love you like a brother,
although we both are one in the same.
Continue to fight and break down walls,
for I know that your smile, will shine so bright.

Keep Moving Forward,
and Never Give Up.
I'll talk to you again,
so long my friend □

The Artist

I paint the canvas,
with all my dreams.
I write the words,
to boost my esteem.

No matter the location.
not even the time.
I paint the canvas,
and share my gleam.

One night

If I can get through a night without you...
I won't need you anymore
I won't blow your phone
Or beg you to open the door
I just need one night
Without picking a fight
Or questioning my right
I just need one night
To feel like I am enough
One night

If I can get through a night without you...
I won't need you anymore
I won't blow your phone
Or beg you to open the door
I just need one night
Without picking a fight
Or questioning my right
I just need one night
To feel like I am enough

Dark Depths

Dive deep below
Come see what goes down at night
It's no longer a vision
And no longer a dream
Dive deep below
See what's beneath the surface
Do they sleep at night?
Or do they roam in the dark?
Does the moonlight hit the top?
Or does darkness follow till the sunrise
Dive deep below
Come see what goes down at night
Adventure awaits your journey
Let's coast to our destination
Dark Depths
Let's coast to our destination

~~Cancellation~~

I move in silence,
like a thief in the night.
It used to be my hinderance,
now it's my strength

I shift over to the corner,
and block out the sounds.
The music is a loud performer,
these are not your stomping grounds.

I am not your kind,
I'm very unorthodox.
I feel the paradigm shift,
I feel the panic in my eyes.

People see the worry,
they feel the anxiety rise.
I'm bubbling up inside,
I could explode at any time.

Move away from me,
don't come close.

I don't aspire a true loves touch.
I deny your compassion.

I'm on the edge,
I'm about to blow.
Give me my headphones,
time to stay low.

Passionate Trepidation

This next set of poems are dedicated to the recognition and elimination of fear. We all fear something in our lives. There is not one person who is considered immune.

During these times of unrest and uncertainty our anxieties can be heightened to a point where we struggle to maintain our composure.

Fear can also be an indicator of which things in our lives need to be addressed. When I wrote these poems I was in a place where certain things in the news and on social media caused my fears to increase.

The greatest thing about my anxiety is the next set of thought-provoking poetry that was birthed from the uncertainty that I felt.

Enjoy!

I See

I see a world of people full of fear.
I see the wise being silent.
I see the fools being spoken.
I see the pain on people's faces.
I see the weight on people's backs.
I see the pressure in people's hearts.
I see the rich live poor.
I see the poor dream about being rich.
I see the happy be neglected.
I see the sadness be reflected.
I see people's ego desperately be protected.
I see opportunity bang on empty doors.
I see empty doors widen with opportunity.
I see the innocent become... not so innocent
anymore.
I see all things.
All the things my eyes can see, what we call real.
Above and beyond all things that I see,
I see, because I feel.

Black Lives Matter

Every time I pass a cop car,
my heart begins to race.
I question if I'm Next,
and worry who's Next.

Interactions with them can be deadly,
it can also be a fatality.
"All cops are nice,"
"They're genuine and kind,"
I'll believe it when I see it
And my community are no longer victims

The smallness of my community does not hinder
my chances, of a beat down from the top guys.
Police brutality does discriminate,
that fact hangs over my head.

I notice the opposite race,
and immediately tense up inside.
Their age doesn't discriminate,
their lies never fall on deaf ears.

It's hard to trust others,
I choose to not be in public.
The color of my skin is powerful,
My power can get me killed.

In public I stay aware,
my head is on a swivel.
Anything can take me out.
One wrong look and that's the end.

I sympathize with those in pain,
from the hate and ignorance of others.
How can one be so hateful?
And oppress those who want equality.

We were all born equal.
We have God given rights.
Society continues to hold us down.
Our president doesn't care.

I wish there was love
I wish there was respect
I wish there was empathy
For the ones with no opportunity
They live in the projects
Area polluted with violence
The War on Drugs was just a Lie,
to keep us down for the count.

Together we rise,
every single morning.

To chase our purpose,
and ignite change.

What should we do?
How do we fix this?
How do we invoke change?
How can we come together?

Stand up
Vote
Take ownership
Be accountable
Love one another
Love yourself
Fight
Spread peace
Dare to be different
Dare to be unique
Don't Stop
Keep Moving
Win
Repeat.
Black Lives Matter

For What I Fear

The world I live in has last control
It embraces me, then suffocates me,
Like a burnt out smoke of charcoal
That used to rage with a memory.

Dreams slowly began to drown
In a world that has lost control,
Hunting, killing, and burning down
The old lies that once told to my soul.

Inside a graveyard of broken hours
All I have known seems unclear,
Yet I set down the flowers,
To live for what I fear.

Cold Winds and Cool Breezes

Ever since a cold wind blew   one night
and crept into my body as I slept
and bounced around until it found unrest in my
breath
I have frozen in my steps.
my strides have stopped stomping right and left.
I'm no longer comfortable in the bed I once slept.
I no longer hold on to those secrets I once kept.
It is all gone, there is no weight on my chest.
I am as lonely as a mother with an empty nest.
My doves and loves are gone my nest is next.
My place I lay.
My case I rest
cold winds and cool breezes

Gazelle vs Lion

Motivated by FEAR
Motivated by HUNGER
These intense emotions
Are what makes them tick

In your fight or flight instance,
when you are driven by great emotions.
Will you run on FEAR?
Or run by HUNGER?

One

One serious moment
One thoughts display
One forgotten memory
Move on

Isolation

I feel like I don't deserve love
I'm not worthy of it
The whole world is hanging over me,
preparing to crush my peace.
I feel the weight of my emotions,
hanging on my shoulders.
I wish to be understood.
Someone who feels my pain.
I feel like I'm a burden,
and no one wants to play.
I have no answers for my guilt,
I hang my head low.
My gut tells me to run away,
and never be seen again.
Hiding under the covers feels very smart,
will it take me far?
Locked in a room away from others,
seems like the best route.
This cloud is looming over,
I feel the storm coming.
It's time to take care,
and lock myself away.

Colors

Colorful **trees**, glimmering and shining,
Colorful skies, alternate with timing,
Colorful **flowers**, blooming and elegant,
Colorful **seas**, dark but extravagant

-

Colorful love, vibrant and dancing,
Colorful eyes, dreaming and prancing,
Colorful earth, breathing and smiling,
Colorful me, drowning but trying.

Tired this Time

Sometimes a break can help the best
But usually eventually leads to no rest
Now it's time to get on with the show
Show the world how much you know
Suddenly silently in creeps the doubt
Paralyzed pondering what you're about
Questions hopefully answered in time
Until then no worries, enjoy the climb

And then I Flew

I could be a river through a mountain.
running through its darker woods
or I could be water on a tabletop
gathering myself before I jump.
And then I Flew

Grey

Love is not simply one color
We continue to chase each other
Sometimes we're in sync,
Other times we stray.

It's red and blue
It's me and you
And once in awhile...
Grey comes through too.

Impairment

Winds burning wet eyes,
We gaze across frozen trees
-"Let's never go back."

Leadership

I wonder what lies?
Between those soft orange eyes.
They turn brown with anger,
they become wild in danger.

You run the pride,
You never turn and hide.
You pave the way,
you molded the future with clay.

I wonder what lies?
When your eye is on the prize.
You are the protector,
and turn into a collector.

You walk with confidence,
your silence is captivating.
You pounce when you're ready,
you lead by example.

I wonder what lies?
When you sit and spy.
Hiding behind the warm tall grass,
threatening to break your enemies clear glass.

On paper you are intimidating,
your size is unobtainable.
Everyone around fears you,
I admire your presence.

I wonder what lies?
Between those eyes.
I want to enter your mind,
and watch you on your grind.

I aspire to intake the peace you bring,
and inherit your roar,
to run my bloodline.

Head of the Table

This is my yard
I run these streets
Obey my one command
Or get run down
I am the Chief
You listen to me
Don't say a word
Don't question my lesson
This is tough love
I hope you understand
The Head of the Table
Don't touch my plate

Head of the Table II

Force my hand...
and I will make sure you understand...
who I am...
The Tribal Chief.
The Head of the Table.
The Best of the Best.
The Provider.
The Protector.
The Gentleman.
The Giver.
The Taker.
Give the family my love.

Passionate Introspection

I am a person who is affected by nature. I obeserve and take in all that it has to offer. When I feel stressed and overwhelmed, the calm, cool breeze and the rustle of the trees help me feel alive.

As a water sign, I love to be near the ocean and get lost in the waves. I am reminded that my life is a beautiful reflection of the Earth in which I reside.

Sometimes it is best to take a step back from everything and simply observe your surroundings.

I have found that when I am frustrated or filled with emotion there is nothing better than to just sit and feel. Your senses of touch, taste, feel, and smell are reminders that you are still alive.

These next set of poems were written during my times of introspection and deep thought.

Roots (Haiku)

Sprouting underground.
Waiting to breathe the surface.
Roots before branches.

Observations

I thought it was a terrible trait to have,
now I'm grateful for my insightful spirit.
I sit and reflect,
on what the world has become.
I don't say a word,
I pick and choose my battles.
To see what is worth fighting for,
and if this hill is worthy of my presence.
I observe high energy,
and notice that's not for me.
I observe and discover sadness,
and I empathize with their spirit.
I move myself in the corner,
and choose to protect my peace.
It's a constant game of tug of war,
to choose what's right for me.
I see people play checkers,
I choose to play chess.
My quiet energy can be seen as weakness,
I choose to walk in silence.
Sometimes the silence can become too much,
and I open my mouth to speak.
I question if people will understand,
the words behind my emotions.
If they perceive my thoughts as lies,
I shut down and cannot talk.
My silence is a strength,
I no longer view it as a weakness.
I have the power to choose my behavior,
and act on my emotions, when the time is right.

Observations II (Haiku)

keep your ears open
fasten your eyes to stay wide
and keep your mouth shut

Thoughts From An Empath

Tired eyes,
Shortcrust pies,
Marmite skies,
Lavender spies,

.

Uncomfortable growth,
Tight-gripped choke,
Urban smoke,
Soul so broke.

.

Fresh green grass,
Heart of glass,
New contrast,
Proud Empath

Drifting

The waves overtake us
    Blue and white against the boat
        Touch the coolness and feel the air

The Five Senses

I look at you

But not with my eyes

Not how I see everyone else

I see you with my other senses

I smell you

You smell like the sun's heat on fresh laundry

You smell like earth, a handful of fresh dirt

I hear you, your soft breathing

I imagine your breathing in different scenarios

Fast, with a soft hum as you feel my lips against you

I like this scenario the best

Or quiet, slow

You're sleeping, this one makes me feel safe, happy

I touch you

You're warmth, your skin is soft

This is what I long for most

Nothing special

Just to touch your skin and feel that you're hear

That you're real, and you are

I taste you

You're sweet, like candy

Reminds me of being a child

You're also bitter, as most people are

There's something there I couldn't have seen with

my eyes

But that's okay, everyone tastes bitter sometimes

Finally, I see you

In a way I couldn't have before

I know you without my eyes now

Your beauty is consistently throughout

You are the epitome of a woman

The woman of my five senses

Radiance

I wish you could stay forever,
and you wouldn't fade away.
Your warmth radiates my body,
the atmosphere uplifts my soul.

All good things must come to an end,
and I'll miss the feelings you brought me inside.
You come every year just like a good friend,
Now you fade away, and I miss what you provide.

You bring me peace,
You bring me joy,
Running with you provided me a release,
You kept me energized like a child with a new toy.

Sunsets were the best with you,
You painted the skies with orange and pink.
I can't forget that deep dark blue,
On days like that, I made sure not to blink.

Your leaves have fallen, and now you're so bare.
I search over and over, hoping to see you cling.

I'll tend to you with love,
I'll tend to you with care.
Soon we'll meet like doves,
And fly high above.

Dark grey skies await my future,
Sharp cold air will pierce my face.
I wish I had a drop of humor,
To create a happy place.

You always return when the time is right,
And my spirit becomes enlightened.
I'll fly my kite in the bright sunlight,
and will no longer dare to be frightened.

Our goodbye is temporary,
you may return soon.
Please return in February,
But don't be too hot like June.

Your warmth has died,
yet I know you will rise.
I'll return to you and leave from inside,
to let you in, with wide brown eyes.

Warmth

Laughter, smiles, joy, that's what warms my heart.
A simple hello, with a bright and joyful smile, warms my
spirit and fills my heart.

The way they run, when they see my face.
The way they hide, to try and surprise me.
Their mischievous ways, of making me laugh, that's
what warms my heart.
A happy conversation, a sad conversation, a mad
conversation, or even a silly conversation, I look back on
those days, and reflect with a smile,
that's what warms my heart.
Whether I feel happy, or mad,
sad or lost,
I know I can find that one child,
that is able to warm my heart.
My heart is now huge, from the warmth they bestowed
upon me,
Now it's turned to golden, with just a simple touch.

49

Autumn

Orange.
   Yellow.
      Red.
        Green.

Please don't forget Purple and brown.
   The skies are painted with majestic colors.
      The sun shines brights and radiates ones soul.

A long deep forest,
   with trees booming high.
      Their leaves have fallen,
        Feel the crunch as you walk.

I wish to climb those trees.
   And reach to touch the sky.
      I'd like to be a bird for one day,
        And fly to my destination.

All good things do come to an end,
   This is true by 12-21.
      I'll miss the comfort that you brought me
        each day.
            I will see you next year when I feel
            your breeze.

The Arctic Blues

The cold pierces my heart.
It's no walk in the park.
The weather shakes my mind,
and makes me want to hide.

A new desire has opened my eyes.
I want to make a journey,
into the unknown.

I question my sanity and wishing to go there.
Who would want to travel there?
The degrees is always negative.
The sun never likes to play.

It's cold 24/7
I can feel the ice beneath my toes
There is no warmth
The sun won't help

Yet to step there would be an ultimate thrill

The pictures there captivate me,
The snow is awe inspiring
I can't forget the sea life
Not even that giant white bear

To shake a penguins hand
And feel his slippery flippers
I wonder if they dance and flap all day
Then catch some fish as the sun begins to drop

Global warming is truly a killer
Threatening to make my dream obsolete
I refuse to let this dream go to waste
I will step foot into the Unknown.

December Skies

Occasional patches
Of cerulean blue
spread hope as they cut through
endless waves of heavy grey.
December skies
lull you outside
under the false semblance
of kinder days
I always freeze up on days like these;
heavy jacket, no gloves,
Yet I still feel the ice
Light feathers soar above
in December skies.
This sun is about to set,
broken skin shivering in my pockets
Not even the glow of the moon
can save these December skies

What Happens?

What happens to everyone
in the winter
when the days stay short
and the sun gets small
the trees are naked
not a leaf in sight
the atmosphere is cold
and very dark
the snow is bright
the ice hangs low
the water drips down
and the pond is solid.

What happens to everyone?

Does anyone know?

Where in the Winter
does everyone go?

Sour then Sweet

I like you when you're yellow
It inspires a taste of mellow
You're amazing when you're red
It doesn't make me shred
I love you when you're blue
My spirit becomes anew
I don't favor you in green
I prefer you to be unseen
You're deplorable in orange
I find that very boring

Chocolate Chip Cookie

It kills me inside,
That you are so tasty
And so delicious
You're also very sugary
And everything I want
But in this great life,
where my lifestyle should be nutritious.
And my diet must be well balanced,
I can't have you.
Even if I want you.
But when the time is right,
And I have enough funds to buy you.
We will meet again,
and you will be mine.

Saturday Night

Night has fallen
I sit here alone
No distractions around
No assignments to complete
No loud music
To block out the vibes
Only soft music
And nostalgia of what was
I put my thoughts on paper
To see if they are real
I read the words of the great philosophers
So I do not self destruct
I may find a nice spot
To eat some good food
Self-care is key
To finding ultimate happiness
I have Saturday's when I'm happy
I have Saturday's when I'm sad
Sometimes I feel angry
Other times I loathe others
The lights are off as I lay in bed
My bed is warm
And my room is at the right temperature

I'm thankful for what my Lord has given me
The art of literature
Is a beautiful gift
To come from a man
Of all creators

Taking off the Train Wheels

Taking off the Training Wheels,
can't you see.

These words don't conceal,
how I feel.

These words aren't sealed,
not locked away.

They're shackled through chains,
And connected through my veins.

Taking off the Training Wheels,
can't you see

These thoughts run wild,
They run side by side.

The words become unhinged,

Like I'm a lunatic fringe.
I'm losing my mind,
I feel cold inside.

They misunderstand, the smiles and laughs,
And take the kindness, for granted.

I don't understand my reason,
So it's hard to take in the new season.

Taking off the Training Wheels,
can't you see.

I feel untamed,
and ashamed of what has become.

This is my life,
The life I live.

I will no longer live in strife,
but lead a victorious life.

Taking off the Training Wheels,
can't you see.
These words don't conceal,
how I feel.

This is my story that you are reading,
My wheels have now spun off,
Now it's off to the races.
Taking of the Train Wheels

Taking off the Training Wheels,
can't you see.

These words don't conceal,
how I feel.

These words aren't sealed,
not locked away.

They're shackled through chains,
And connected through my veins.

Passionate Silence

Have you ever felt unheard or unseen? These feelings can be the most painful experiences that anyone has ever had.

There are times when I feel silenced and lost. These are generally moments in my life when I have to sit and reflect to be reminded of my true purpose and my calling.

We are not placed on this Earth to be happy and entertained. We are all here for a solid purpose. I endeavor in this lifetime to find my purpose and to pursue it with vigor.

I know that I am not alone in my feelings. I know that someone out there has had moments in their lives where they felt like they were speaking but no one was listening, or they were standing in front of a crowd only to feel invisible.

I dedicate these next set of poems to those who feel silenced.

Race

I turn my head left
I turn my head right
Wishing I was that person
The one with the smile

I walk around the room,
and I feel all alone
I feel like a zombie,
my movements are lethargic.

I see happiness to my left
I see joy to my right
Sometimes I see pain
Sometimes I see sadness

I pick up peoples backpacks and take on their
baggage.
I'm the one that provides encouragement.
Sometimes I need some too.

I see us racing side by side.
We're both neck and neck.
I want to win the World Cup
But my batteries are dead and I'm going to drop.

Can you hear me now?

I have a cloud.
That follows me every day.
It grows so big, it attracts a crowd.

It's big and grey.
Sometimes it's white.
Other times it thunders
I wish the tears would delay.

I'm told to express myself.
And let my emotions in.
Sometimes it becomes too much,
And I feel like departing inside.

The cloud is about to burst,
I hear the thunder crackling.
The roar of thunder is booming
Can someone hear my cry?

Self-Critical

I bottle everything up, and hide my emotions inside.
I pretend to be okay.
It's not healthy, I know, but I don't want to be a
burden.
I don't want to have people worry about me. It's not
fair to them, you know?
It's just me. I mean, if it was someone else, I'd
understand, but not me. You get it now?
I wake up every day, and I'm thankful it's a new
day.
Then something will come and trigger me, and then
my mood will go South.
I have my days where I let go of the pain.
I bury them inside and try to cover it.
Then I have those days where they rise to the
surface.
And my feelings become too much,
they give way from my crutch.
I'm in my own head.
I'm in my own little world.
Sometimes I wish to escape.

Other times I'm strapped in the chair.
I feel like people don't understand.
I feel like I'm better off being gone.
I wish that I could run and hide,
But my purpose is bigger than that.
I look in the mirror and find a grey cloud.
It's alright raining,
Sometimes it is just cloudy.
I hope and pray for sunny days.
Right now it's rainy,
I'm forced to acknowledge that.
Does it make me a failure if I quit for a day?
Does it make me a failure if I quit for three days?
I feel like a failure if I do decided to rest.
I'm supposed to be a man,
real men don't cry.
I question my purpose.
I question what's the point of it all.
Every day I feel sad.
Who wants to be around me?
I walk into a room and I put on my happy face.
When the day comes to an end, I take my mask off.
I don't just remove my face mask,
I remove the mask that I wish I could be.
The cloud is about to burst, I hear the thunder
crackling.
The roar of thunder is booming
Can someone hear my cry?

Over analyzing

Stressing myself out.
Driving myself crazy.
Going through the motions, and creating self doubt.
My mind is in chains, and gradually becoming lazy.
No I'm not crazy,
just starting to get shaky.

The anticipated result was better than expected.
All of my expectations were met with reception.
Instead of wallowing and feeling dejected,
I countered the play and made my interception.

All the Same

I want to paint myself
On the walls and the leaves
Of the downtown café
And the poisonous trees
I want to run through the forest
Like the Artic wolves
Want to smell the ocean water
And also take in the roses

I want to wash myself
in the streetlight stars,
Want to swim through the wind
As I ride atop the cars
Want to kiss each page
Of a street vendor's Bible
So when I kiss a lover
I become a disciple

I want to share myself
Like a passed-down fable

As I spread like butter
Across the dining room table
Want to ride with the top down
And let the wind take me in
I no longer want to be lost
I just want to be found

But of all these things
I do only when I dream
I want to shout from the rooftops
And boost my self esteem
For the world is in order
Yet everything is so untamed
Yes I want what I want
I want our world to become acclaimed

Drowning

Sadness
Loneliness
Anger
Confusion

Contempt
Melancholy
Sorrow
Trouble

Misery
Unhappiness
Heaviness
Pain

Hopelessness
Helplessness
Drowning
Help

When will it be over?
Will this pain ever stop?

Will this confusion go away?
Or will I always feel pain?

My heart feels heavy.
It feels like I'm drowning.
I want to reach and grasp the surface,
but the water is too heavy,
too strong and powerful.

In my heart I know I'm better than this.
In my mind I know I'm stronger than this.
So tell me why do I feel this way?
Why is my mind playing tricks with me?

My arms are tired.
My legs are tired.
My body is tired.
My mind is tired.

My head pounds with pain.
My brain rattles anxiously.
My heart feels weak.
My spirit feels dead.

The world is surrounded with water,
and I feel like I cannot survive.
Every time I reach the surface to breath,
The monster comes and pulls me down.

My struggles and problems are hard to shape.
I wish I was super man,
with a magic cape.

My inner circle doesn't give a damn,
will I withstand and speak on this again?

Gone

You're dead to me,
you mean nothing to me.

Thought you was my mans,
but it was all smoke and mirrors.

You didn't respond when I needed you the most,
I guess you always thought of me as a joke.

I wonder what you say behind my back,
that I'm weak,
and that I just don't crack.

I refuse to croak anymore,
I refuse to doubt myself.

No more,
no more doubting myself.

No more questioning my traits and abilities.
You're dead to me,
you mean nothing to me.

You contact me when it's convenient for you,
yet you turn a blind eye the second I go blue.

What am I to you?
I guess I'm nothing.

It was all smoke and mirrors,
and it was all a lie.

So no more,
no more doubting myself.

No more questioning my traits and abilities.

I am ME,
I am who I am.

No response,
no problem.

You're dead to me,
you mean nothing to me.

Tick Tock

One day, one month, one year.
You still fill my "day-to-day."
And now I find myself unable
To handle all of these conversations
With all of these meaningful jokes
They say "Time heals all wounds."
So, I haven't looked away from the clock
It goes "Tick Tock"
Much like a habit,
I want to call your name
But like the hands of time
We keep running past each other.

There'll be days

There'll be days when the world is grand
And you can't wait to go out there

There'll be days when the insecurity burns
and you can't stand your hands

There'll be days you have to scream it all out
and wonder all night if this is what life should be
about

There'll be days when you can't get out of bed
and you lay sinking without an end

There'll be days when you can't sit down
and you wish for the feeling of your favorite chair

There'll be days of joy no doubt
and when he comes don't look down
Breath it in and enjoy the air
There'll be days

There'll be days when the world is grand

And you can't wait to go out there

There'll be days when the insecurity burns
and you can't stand your hands

There'll be days you have to scream it all out
and wonder all night if this is what life should be
about

There'll be days when you can't get out of bed
and you lay sinking without an end

There'll be days when you can't sit down
and you wish for the feeling of your favorite chair

There'll be days of joy no doubt
and when he comes don't look down
Breath it in and enjoy the air

Pain

I'm told to keep my head up,
and to keep fighting for what is right.
The pain in my heart is real,
I miss you very much.

I wish I didn't have to go through this,
and feel this terrible loss.
I want to sleep and stay like that,
and wake up from this terrible dream.

My heart is hurting very much,
it's as if it's being crushed.
When you left this world on that sunny day,
I think you took me with you.

You'd probably hate for me to feel like this,
to feel this pain and hurt.
I wish my heart could have some joy,
but who knows if I'll be the same.

I wish a friend could feel my pain,
no not in a negative way.

I long for companionship and love from my friends,
to ease my hurt and fill my pain.

How do I continue to pickup the pieces?
Where do I go from here?
Everyone wants me to be strong,
but how do I heal my broken heart?

I miss you Dad and that is true,
I wish you were home with me.
I'm happy that you have wings and you can fly,
but I miss you still with a broken heart.

Our Ship

I want to build a ship,
A ship for you and me,
A ship to ride the waves,
A ship to sail the seas.

Something to last the storm,
Something a bit crazy,
Something to look at,
Something pretty.

I tired so hard.
I didn't see,
The holes you made,
The nails left free.

The storm came and the waves rose,
I could only flee.
The ship went down like a stone,
Back into the sea.

Your promises hollow,
Your vows empty,
To think you cared,
Like I did was silly

I did my part,

And then some more,
Guess it was only me,
Doing the chores.

What did I do?
What did I say?
To deserve this wound,
To deserve this ache.

I just wanted a ship,
A ship for you and me,
A ship to ride the waves,
A ship to sail the seas.

The Lonely Introvert

I walk alone on this long dark road.
It seems so long.
And feels so cold.

These words help me unload.
When all seems lost.
Although I doubt my ability,
my soul is clear and bold.

Will it always be this way?
Crouching in this corner?
Or will I shed my shell?
And embrace the sheer unknown.

I find fulfillment when I rise from bed.
My list sits out waiting to see what's in order.
We get to 11:00, and I could be done.
My energy is dead, or sometimes it's sparks up.

I want to be noticed
I want to be seen
Other times I hide,
and sink down to my abyss.

"Pick me!" I think.
"Look down," if the anxiety rises.
"Stay quiet," so it stays professional.

"Move to the corner," and hide those fears.

Long car rides are the best.
The music blasts high,
the wind hits my skin.
I feel at peace.
I feel free.

Removing myself from a situation,
even when all seems lost
I slowly find my groove,
when I love myself from within.

"The spotlight is on me."
"Run away and hide."
Or is my brain telling me stories?
Deceiving my thoughts into a lie.

I'm the dusty old book.
That hangs in the back.
If you dust me off well,
you might learn something new.

I aspire for quiet time.
A room full of noise makes my world go turning.
The mountain called life seems hard to climb.
Instead of fear,
I choose to accept it.

"Comparison is the thief of joy"
"Envy is the root of all evil"
No one follows me down this road.
This is my spot,
I walk alone.

Passionate Faith

Now faith is the substance of things hoped for, the evidence of things not seen. – Hebrews 11:1

True faith is most prevalent during times of petulance and fear. I am proud of the faith that I have gained during this journey. After everything that I have experienced, I found joy on my journey and hope for a brighter future.

Sometimes we must go through the darkness to find the brighter days. My brighter days are here in this moment. I have found my purpose and my passion. For that I feel blessed and honored.

This next set of poems reflects that faith and hope that I currently feel. This does not mean that my life is absent of drama or pain, but I know that my faith will keep me walking towards my destination with less trepidation.

If things are not going well for you in this very moment, I invite you to lean on your faith and meditate on these poems.

Hope

Days become weeks.
Weeks become months.
Months become years.
Hearing this makes me shriek.

Spring becomes Summer.
Summer becomes Fall.
Fall becomes Winter.
Can I really withstand it all?

This past summer was a bummer.
Beginning Fall was a problem.
Will this winter hinder my growth?
Or will I paint the sky with color?

Winter causes pain and suffering.
Spring welcomes opportunity and growth.
April showers bring forth May Flowers,
Shall I take a new approach?

Bundle up you'll need a coat,
I roll my eyes and skin feels like ice.
Maybe I'll just plan to fail and choke,
"No, no, Bryce, fly to new heights."

Faith inspires discipline.
Discipline furthers growth.
Growth leads to new beginnings.
And new beginnings offers hope.

The Light

Wake up I say.
Shake your mind and unsettle your thoughts.
Drop the rope and walk away.
Raise your head and try again.
Your life is better than being dead.

The rain will stop and the sun will shine.
Specks of color will touch the sky.
Imagine the Fall of beautiful colors,
Orange, red, yellow, and pink.
Envision your future,
being that bright.

You're a light I say,
and that's no lie.
No bs statements,
No fibs and no pre-truths.
Continue to touch the world,
and paint your canvas with a multitude of colors.

Don't be afraid, to take off the training wheels.
For although children always fall,
they always stand back up.

When you fall down and start to cry,
Don't aspire to die,
stand up and soar to fly.

You have the strength of a bear.
The endurance of a cheetah.
The wingspan of an eagle.
And the encouragement of a lion pride.

Get up and roar with your head held high.
Poke your chest out, stick it out like a bird.
Walk towards the light, you're getting closer.
Get ready for the ride,
it's gonna be long and fun.

Pendulum

I wish I had the words to say to you.
I stammer over my words and my tongue gets tied.
I think about you and overthink my thoughts.
I wish I could get over my fears,
to say the words I feel for you.
You're very beautiful,
with a very kind heart.
A heart of gold,
That I believe mimics mine.
Every time I see you,
You run through my mind.
I search for your car,
and hope you'll be there.
When I see it in the open,
my heart flutters like eagles.
And an emptiness fills my mind,
whenever you aren't around.
I wish I could believe in myself.
To say that I'm worth talking to you.
Maybe someday that time will come,
I pray that God heals my mind.
If it's meant to be,

I'll treat you with love.
If it's not meant to be,
I pray for strength.
Your spirit is captivating,
and I respect your drive.
You are very encouraging,
with a kind and beautiful soul.
You deserve a guy,
who can give you peace.
Maybe it's time I ought to respect myself.
So maybe it's time,
for me to say goodbye.
And close the door,
on a love that may never be.

Go Getters

We plant our feet and off we go
To tackle some barriers and knock down doors
Winter seems horrendous because of the snow
But like a pride of lions, we'll push them down with
roars

Our feats of strength may bring us danger
It effects our minds and makes us collapse
But we're not prisoners shackled in a chamber
Our weapons will protect us and we will not snap

We see opportunities there
We see them far away
Protect us with care
And bring us a new day

The sun looks bright
It powers use to move
It provides us with insight
On which path to choose

The light sometimes fades

And diminishes into the abyss
Just like an ace of spades
People turn and drop amiss

It's hard to find encouragement
When the night seems low
We work together in this entanglement
We are our hero's

Along this empty road
We link hands and walk together
You can count on me when you need to unload
You are forever my go getter.

Remembrance

I miss your walk.
I miss the way you talked.
I miss the way you parked your car.
I miss the clothes you used to where.
I miss the way you sat in your chair.
I miss the way you'd call us to come eat.
I miss pressing your name in my contacts.
I miss being able to text you.
I miss the emojis you sent my way.
I miss being able to call you.
I miss your smile.
I miss your laugh.
I miss you way too much.
I will never forget you.
I will always see you.
I will always feel your spirit.
I still miss you.
I will miss you tomorrow.
I will miss you for always and eternity.

The Pride

We walk together in this pride.
We stand side by side, and never steer away.
Our loyalty is clear.
Our blood runs deep.
My brothers are bold.
And my sisters are courageous.

We never turn our backs,
when we are told to kill our kind.
My loyalty for my pride,
will never ever die.

My lionesses is peaceful.
She co leads the pack.
Her strength is endearing.
Her strength gives me power.

We're coming for you prey.
You think you can kill us, but you have no strength.
We'll break you down,
brick by brick.
Then move for the kill,

and steal our bite.

This pride is strong.
We all stick together.
No weapons will fade us.
Watch for my roar.

The Chief

When the heat is high
And the leaves go dry
The streams flow low
And the pack walks slow

Mirages vivify
Laughs the all seeing eye
The whole pack dies
And the lone wolf survives
The Chief

When the heat is high
And the leaves go dry
The streams flow low
And the pack walks slow

Mirages vivify
Laughs the all seeing eye
The whole pack dies
And the lone wolf survives

Relax

Be silent.
Be still.
Calm down.
Relax.

Breath easy.
Deep breaths.
Easy eyes.
Relax.

Be peaceful.
Stay calm.
Be mindful.
Relax.

Breath in.
Breath out.
Don't quit.
Relax.

Eyes closed.
Ears wide.
Mouth shut.
Relax.

Crossed fingers.
Crossed legs.
Smile lightly.
Relax.

I got this.
You got this.
We got this.
Relax.

You'll Never See It Coming

You'll Never See It Coming,
I promise you it's true.
It comes at you so fast,
you'll never know what hit you.
One minute you're two and your counting to three,
the next minute you're five, and you're running to
be alive.

You'll Never See It Coming,
I promise you it's true.
It comes at you so fast,
you'll never know what hit you.
One minute you're eleven and you're opening a
locker,
The next minute you're thirteen, you're finally a
teen!

You'll Never See It Coming,
I promise you it's true.
It comes at you so fast,
you'll never know what hit you.
One minute your fourteen, with your earphones in
the back seat.
The next minute you're sixteen, riding in the fast
lane.

You'll Never See It Coming,
I promise you it's true.
It comes at you so fast,
you'll never know what hit you.
One minute you're seventeen, maybe eighteen,
maybe nineteen.
You receive your diploma with a tight firm
handshake.
The next moment you're twenty two, graduating
with a degree.

You'll Never See It Coming,
I promise you it's true.
It comes at you so fast,
you'll never know what hit you.
One minute you're, twenty five, working your
career.
The next minute you're down the aisle, saying I Do.

You'll Never See It Coming,
I promise you it's true.
It comes at you so fast,
you'll never know what hit you.

One minute you're thirty, with a growing family of your own.
The next minute you're forty, with a Masters and Doctorate.

You'll Never See It Coming,
I promise you it's true.
It comes at you so fast,
you'll never know what hit you.
One minute you're in the drivers seat, driving your children around.
The next minute you're in the passengers seat, gripping the seat for dear life.

You'll Never See It Coming,
I promise you it's true.
It comes at you so fast,
you'll never know what hit you.
One minute you're fifty, celebrating your life.
The next minute you're sixty five, it's time to retire.

You'll Never See It Coming,
I promise you it's true.
It comes at you so fast,
you'll never know what hit you.
One minute you're seventy five, watching you grand and great grands.
The next minute you're seventy nine, your fiftieth wedding anniversary.

You'll Never See It Coming,
I promise you it's true.

It comes at you so fast,
you'll never know what hit you.
One minute you're meeting friends, building your
inner circle.
The next minute you're saying goodbye, sometimes
with a smile,
and sometimes with a tear.

Coincide

Ego is one side, pride is another
Happiness is life, discipline is a brother
Struggle is temporary, victory is certain
Set your mindset
and weaken your burden
From life's problems, we build important experience
To grow strong, defy inner demons
and build resilience
To conquer the world

Purpose

I'm meant to do work today
I'm called to flap my wings
Although I'm too small,
my family believes in me.
My wings may be broken,
But I have strength inside.
My feet may hurt,
But I am still walking.
Mother's going to push me now,
The ground seems so far.
I have no choice but to fly away,
So here goes nothing..

Success

What does success mean to you?
Is it mastering the ability to tie your shoes?
Is it solving that puzzle by using index clues?
Or is it creating purple with red and blue?
What does success mean to you?

What does success mean to you?
Is it Saturday nights hanging with the crew?
Or finding the power to start something new?

What does success mean to you?
Is it turning a new leaf and changing your life?
In order to do that, you must remove remove strife.

What does success mean to you?
Is it believing in yourself?
Or is it placing all your accolades on your success shelf?
What if it's believing that you are the best?
Or like a young baby bird, taking flight out of your inner nest?
So I ask again, what does success mean to you?

What does success mean to you?
Is it reaching for the stars?
Is it not only setting the bar, but raising the bar?
Or is it knowing that you can?
So maybe one day you can be the man?

The man has done all of this.
He set the bar, he raised the bar, and he became
the bar.
He reached for the stars, and soared past Mars.

The man became the master of his own destiny.
God just gave him the tools to perfect his craft.
The man is perfection.

The man accomplished dreams that were
unobtainable.
To teach us, that all dreams are obtainable.

So what does success mean to you?

Pressing Forward, Never Back

I've paid the piper, now must dance the dance.
Waltzing forward in a trance.
Demons pleading "Be still, it's easy"
"Please relax, rewind, you need me!"
But I never have, and I never will.
I'm moving forward, you're such a shill.

Now I've paid already so step aside.
I hear the music, it's time to glide.

Imaglnation

I want to go to this world,
called Imaglnation.

Where I am a different kind of breed,
And will always continue to exceed.

In Imaglnation, I am always the best,
and everyone else, they are put to rest.

I try to fade the negativity,
and make it go away.

Maybe I should have listened to my mother,
and leave it all astray.

Imaglnation is where my mind runs free,
I fly like a bee,
and sing like birds in a tree.

The sun shines everyday,
with a perfect temperature of 73,
and life is just simple
and everything, is as it seems.

So this is ImagInation,
the perfect world that I have created.

So if you see me glazed over,
and in another world,
know that I am in ImagInation
Where I, am the controller.

Gratitude 🙏

Thank you for my life.
Thank you for my mother.
Thank you for my brother.
Thank you for my family.

Thank you for the clothes on my back.
Thank you for the socks on my feet.
Thank you for the shoes on my feet.
Thank you for the warmth that comforts my body.

Thank you for my running car.
Thank you for the heat that warms my soul on a
chilly December.
Thank you for the air that cools my body on a hot
July.

Thank you for my friends.
Thank you for my acquaintances.
Thank you for my best friends.
Thank you for my cousins.

Thank you for forgiveness.
Thank you for love.

Thank you for mercy.
Thank you for grace.

Thank you for my hobbies.
Thank you for my writing.
Thank you for the books of mine.
Thank you for my love of coloring.

Thank you for my peace.
Thank you for my smooth voice.
Thank you for my quietness.
Thank you for protecting me.

Thank you for my drive.
Thank you for my creativity.
Thank you for my goals.
Thank you for my purpose.

Thank you for your love.
Thank you for your mercy.
Thank you for your grace.
Thank you for your patience.

Thank you for my patience.
Thank you for my kindness.
Thank you for my failures.
Thank you for my lessons.

Thank you for the morning.
Thank you for the evening.
Thank you for the nighttime.
Thank you for waking me up.

Conclusion

Do it with passion or not at all! This collection of poetry has been the epitome of my life's work. Some of these poems were written during a time when I couldn't see what was ahead, but I was determined to pen my feelings and thoughts.

I encourage you to continue to read, write, and create. Find a way to express yourself and just be. We are currently in the throes of a pandemic and emotions are at an all time high.

It is my hope that one of my poems have uplifted and motivated you to a point of peace in these tumultous times.

Thank you for taking the time to embark upon this journey.

Lamond Cedrick Hawkins

September 21,1976 – September14, 2020

September 14, 2020 my father gained his wings.
This was the most difficult time of my life. He was a
good man who loved his family dearly. I will forever
be grateful for his presence in my life. This section
is dedicated to you, Dad. I love you forever!

Love

A Poem for Lamond C. Hawkins

One strong man
A heart of gold
Could be at stubborn times,
but always showed love.
You gave me lots of compassion,
and provided a ton of empathy.
Although your time unfortunately came,
your legacy on Earth will forever be ultimate.
I may have said goodbye on that day,
but the door will never be chained forever.
I'll open it up when the time is right,
and let you in to see your hard work shine.
In loving memory of my loving father.
Happy trails to you, until we meet again.

Cedrick and Lamond Hawkins

Cedrick and Lamond at High School
Graduation 2018

Lamond, Charles Hawkins Sr. (Pop Pop), and
Cedrick at High School Graduation 2018

Cedrick and Charles Hawkins Sr. (Pop Pop)

Cedrick and Joyce Hawkins (Nana Hawkins)

Cedrick and Paulette Creek (Nana Creek)

Dad (Clifton Creek), Kyle, Jordan, and Ced

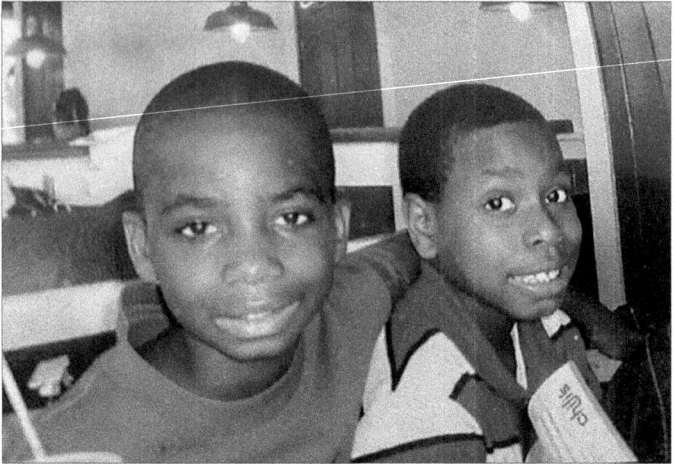

Cedrick Hawkins and AJ Reynolds

Johnathan Brock, RJ Holland, and Cedrick

Edwin Stewart, Cedrick Hawkins, and
Demeetre Creek

Cedrick and Edwin

Cedrick, Auj'Zhanea Brock, and
Demeetre Creek

Cedrick and Kyle Hawkins

About Ced

Cedrick Hawkins is a talented writer, speaker, and scholar. He obtained an Associates of Arts and Science Degree in Communications from the College of Southern Maryland (CSM) in 2020. During his time at CSM his academic achievements included the Honor Roll for all semesters and the Dean's List.

Cedrick is currently working towards a Bachelors of Science Degree in Elementary Education at Bowie State University.

He created the "CedTalks" podcasts which reaches countless individuals weekly. He uses the podcasts as a vehicle to inspire and encourage others.

He is a determined young man and a blessing to his mother. Cedrick is a loyal and protective big brother, a dedicated and loving cousin, and he continues to make his family proud every single day.

www.ingramcontent.com/pod-product-compliance
Lightning Source LLC
Chambersburg PA
CBHW071130090426
42736CB00012B/2078